reimagine
Family
History

Other Books by Devon Noel Lee

21st Century Family Historian

*Power Scrapbooking – Get Caught Up
No Matter Your Scrapbooking Style*

*Create a Family History Scrapbook Digitally
in 12 Simple Steps*

From Metal to Rhinestones: A Quest for the Crown

Other Books by Andrew Lee

How to Fail English with Style

Other Books by Andrew Lee & Devon Noel Lee

A Recipe for Writing Family History

reimagine Family History

Devon Noel Lee
& Andrew Lee

reimagine Family History

Published by Devon Noel Lee

Table of Contents

reimagine Origins

For generations, genealogy sought one thing - to prove lineage. Who begat whom? Are you related to royalty and rulers? Moreover, unless your great aunt died with a large estate and no heirs, she probably did not matter to you.

In the 1800s and 1900s a quest for finding new relatives began. That great aunt became important to tree building. Researchers wanted new names for the pedigree charts and group sheets they compiled and stored in binders, file drawers or scattered across their spare bedroom.

In time, stereotypes developed about genealogy research and rarely was the image flattering. Genealogy was something old people do. Genealogy was laborious or tortuous. Genealogists trampled through poorly maintained cemeteries, scrolled through rolls of microfilm, and wrote long-hand letters to random strangers who might possibly be relatives. The hobby was for strange people with nothing better to do than celebrate finding an original baptism record in a rural church in Canada or Germany. However, times are changing.

Every pastime has its fans in varying degrees. There are those who like to watch baseball, those who casually play baseball, those who play it competitively, and those who are fascinated with stats, the baseball cards, and any number of other mundane details lost to the rest of the world. At the same time, the majority of people have little to no interest in baseball. Genealogy is no different.

There are those stereotypical genealogists who visit cemeteries, archives, and repositories. There are those who conduct genealogy to support their pedigree to gain access to lineage societies. There are also those who collect family names without examining supporting evidence for validation. However, the majority of people could not care less about their family history and avoid genealogical research like the plague.

Despite the continued persistence of negative stereotypes, a subtle paradigm shift has occurred. More people wonder: Is there something more to family history? Is genealogy more than names, dates, and places? Is genealogy only for that weird family member who hoards photos and papers about dead people best forgotten? Should everyone participating in family history be searching for new names?

These questions strike fear into the hearts of some long-time researchers. They complain that few people want to conduct original research and instead ask if a record-set is online and indexed. Another complaint pertains to the lack of research skills among the younger generation. The instant gratification permeating our society demands new names and instant answers without much effort. Many fanatical genealogists fear that genealogy as a pastime and profession will disappear.

Are they right to fear or is the paradigm shift a welcome change? Is better access to records helping or hindering discoveries? To determine the answer, let's examine genealogy throughout history.

Brief History of Genealogy

In ancient times, genealogy focused heavily on establishing lineage. The Bible, Egyptian obelisks, and Chinese Dynasties demonstrate the importance of lineage to ancient civilizations. In many cases, it determined the ruler of empires.

For the most part, genealogy was similar to completing pedigree charts and group sheets to detail who begat whom. At the time, only a small fraction of the people was interested in genealogy, primarily the ruling elite. It was they who had the most to gain from establishing their lineage. For the commoner, there was no benefit, no extra time to put into it, and no extra funds to waste on tracing ancestral relations. For thousands of years, subsistence farmer begat subsistence farmer. Baker begat baker, and shaman begat shaman. Sure there were some exceptions when the blacksmith became a general and later ruler of the empire. These occupational changes were exceedingly rare. We have 5,000 years of recorded history across hundreds of cultures but only a handful of examples where someone whose pedigree did not matter, all of the sudden became necessary.

The tribes of northern Europe have a long history of tracing their kings back to Odin, the hero-god of their culture. While scholars may debate whether there ever was an Odin who lived in Asgard, one thing is constant. Each of the competing tribal chieftains (whether newly crowned or inheriting it through their family) claimed a lineage back to Odin. Compiling a genealogy was a trivial or monumental task depending on what level of accuracy you desired. Few records existed. Few people could read those records. If the chieftain demanded a scribe trace the ruler's lineage back to the gods to solidify his right to rule, then that scribe's survival depended on his ability to find the correct records or create them out of whole cloth. The impossibility of the task is also the reason that no one would likely know what the scribe had produced was inaccurate. Miraculously, scribe after scribe found the links for each of these kings.

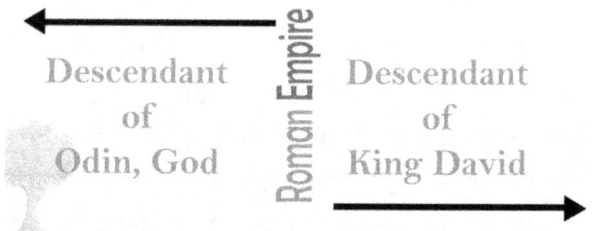

After the fall of the Roman Empire and the introduction of Christianity, the barbarian tribes in Europe sought to bring legitimacy to their new-found nobility. Their conundrum was simple. Their fathers had traced their lineage through the pagan gods back to Odin, but a pagan god could not be the progenitor of Christian rulers. More records were miraculously found! In the ensuing decades and centuries, the Christian European royalty traced their lineage back to show they were related to the royal Jewish line, to the lineage of David. Not only were ancestors grafted into the Odin lines, but the lines intertwined with classical Roman, Greek, and Trojan heroes. Some of these figures are known to be mythological while others or at least the acts attributed to them, are suspect. What the Christian royalty created was a genealogy that included every great ruler known to the western world. How convenient.

Genealogies were kept for nobility, but as kingdoms and empires rose and fell, the nobility became the peasants, and their lineage was lost, forgotten or hidden. By the 16th century, the churches of Europe were keeping records such as baptisms, marriages, and burials. In many places, the church and the government intermingled, and these records became the forerunners of modern civil records. The genealogical value of these records far exceeds what was written about the nobility for three reasons.

First, they were contemporary records of the events. The memories of people dwindle with time, and historical research of any kind should rely on records contemporary to the individuals being studied. Contemporary records preserve the event as it happened or shortly thereafter, which decreases the likelihood of a name or date being misremembered or fabricated.

Second, events were recorded by a disinterested third party. In most cases, the priest or clerk had no reason to make up information. These records were used for taxation and welfare. Accuracy was desired to carry on the ecclesiastical and civil functions.

Third, documents recorded essentially everyone. Since the church was the focal point of society, all people were included in these records. Rich or poor, all received a line in the church book. Without realizing it, the church had started a genealogy of everyone in Europe. When church records were replaced with civil records, they became more comprehensive and reached out to find every person that may have been missed. Other than children who died a few days or weeks after birth, close to 100% of Western Europeans born since 1600 show up in some record collection. But that does not mean they are easy to find.

Thank a Religion

Churches increased the documentation of nearly 100% of Western Europeans since the 1600s

As migrations across Europe and to the new world occurred, many people held on to their recorded heritage. Family genealogies may have been included in the family Bible, but other families lost their lineage records as they migrated. By the 1800s, individuals with some wealth, seeking to re-establish their heritage, would hire professionals. This era of genealogical research was a little better than the nobility of old. If they were lucky, the professional would compile an accurate lineage. However, the professional researchers still had specific knowledge of records and access to archives that most people did not. Verifying their work at the time would be prohibitively expensive. In the past century, several of these compilations were found to be fabricated out of whole cloth. Far too often, these heritage books would link a person to Charlemagne or another historical hero when there was no such documented evidence.

As more and more lineage works were discovered to be fraudulent, genealogical proof came to the forefront. Thus, when genealogy was taught, the need to find documents verifying facts was stressed. If you wanted to record a life event, you needed to have a birth certificate, death certificate, family Bible, or another record to back up the claim. Although the need to provide evidence is important, far too often those people who wished to record an event but did not have a record to verify it (perhaps only someone's memory) felt that they could not write it down and the information was lost.

Genealogical Proof

Standards developed in the
1900s to combat the rise
in fraudulent genealogies.

Another distressing loss of information occurred as governments were overthrown and new people in power sought to cleanse their lands of the undesirables, especially those with noble ancestry. Places like China that previously had excellent genealogical records going back hundreds and even thousands of years saw families destroying their records to save their lives. In the United States, we complain about burned down courthouses. Imagine dealing with a place like Ukraine or Poland whose lands and cities have been laid waste by wars since Napoleon. Genealogical evidence will probably never be available for most of their ancestors.

Even with a push for documentation, the quality of research remained fair at best. Most people working on genealogy were amateurs, who did not always follow a common standard. Today, one could debate whether genealogy standards would rise if only professionals did the work. But, as the number of professional genealogists will never grow to more than a tiny fraction of the population, the way to increase the quality of genealogical work is not to leave it to experts. Education and peer review will improve the quality of genealogy research.

If someone is very lucky, they will have some records that another person interested in their family lines compiled. This record could simply be a family tree drawn on a sheet of lined paper. It could be a collection of pedigree charts and group sheets. Or it could be a scrapbook filled with not only these charts, but with copies of the documents to support the facts on the charts. Collaborating with others will increase the quality of genealogical research.

Something's Missing

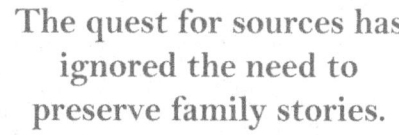

The quest for sources has
ignored the need to
preserve family stories.

Increasing genealogical evidence to create accurate lines of pedigrees is a laudable goal. However, something has been missing since the beginning of genealogy. That something goes back to the questions, "Is there something more to genealogy?" and "Is genealogy more than names, dates, and places?"

If two books are on a shelf, and one is a 900-page story about a family who lived during the French Revolution and the other is a 100-page collection of pedigree charts, birth certificates, and a smattering of journal pages, which one would a person be more likely to pick up and read? Most often the 900-page novel will leave the shelf, even if the quality of the novelist's writing is poor. Charts and records excite only a handful of people. A story that might have been developed from those charts and records is far more attractive. People can envision a setting, emotions, and challenges in a narrative form rather than an outline. If outlines or basic facts were more appealing than stories, we would have no need for tales of Jane Austen, J. R. R. Tolkien, J. K. Rowling.

Despite the knowledge that most people love stories more than charts, genealogy has been slow to adopt the practice of recording the stories as well as the facts. A few educated and passionate people of the past kept wonderful, detailed journals. But if you had a poor ancestor, they probably did not keep a journal, even though they had important stories to share. Few people took the time to write these stories down.

Imagine the value in the details behind the death of a toddler on a German immigrant's farm. The toddler fell into a recently dug well and drowned. When did it happen? Why did no one see the youngster wander off? Who found him? How did the parents react? What was their reaction to the sermon given at the child's funeral that criticized the parents heavily as an 'example' to others? If someone would have written down the answers to these questions, the story could have more depth and accuracy rather than our weak speculation. In this case, the parents were poor and unable to write their side of events. A literate church leader recorded the blasting remarks from the funeral. Someone probably heard the story of the child's death and had the ability to write but did not take the time to record it. Future generations have only a name, birth and death dates, and a location for the event on a pedigree chart. The sermon, if discovered, will paint the family in a negative light. Ultimately, nothing else will be remembered about this poor toddler farm boy and his bereaved parents with the 'traditional' approach to genealogy.

Thankfully, a new wave of interest in family research has changed our perspective of what is important. Genealogy seeks names, dates, and places with the addition of stories that support the details. Emphasis on preserving memories, photos, and keepsakes has increased. Amateur genealogists are now using all of this information, coupled with local and national history, to understand those names on the charts better. The movement is tilting toward preserving memories rather than simply finding new names.

With this paradigm shift, the genealogist stereotype must change. Family historians do not need to be an expert in everything. You can direct the overall research but focus in on the things you enjoy most. Other genealogists will add the things they enjoy collecting most. Together we'll add richer detail into our histories. Collaborating with others, we use our time more efficiently and draw upon wider resources than ever before.

Tools of the 21st century have made family history easier than ever. Instead of spending hours searching through records on microfilm for one name at a library, indexed records online mean we can find whole families and trace them across decades while sitting in our pajamas before breakfast. The pace of research allows us more time to spend on those darn brick walls and tangled tree branches.

Let's use the modern tools and opportunities before us to make a richer, more meaningful book or presentation that can compete for the attention of our children. But before we can do this, we need to reimagine family history. The first step involves reorienting ourselves as to what family history is and the second is to determine what we should be doing.

reimagine Family History

Dig deeper and find more meaning in genealogy research and preservation.

What is Family History?

Before we can understand a definition that says,

"Family history is _____"

let's take a few moments to consider some questions that seem off topic, and then work our way back to a definition.

In the United Kingdom, Australia, Denmark, Czech Republic, and the United States of America, a reality TV show called *Who Do You Think You Are?* is relatively popular. The show follows a celebrity each week as they research their family tree. Have you seen it? If you have, stop and think about why this show is so compelling.

Does it have drama? Yep.

Does it have twists and turns? Yes.

Does it have stories that you can relate to? Absolutely.

In one episode of the American version of the show, country singer Reba McEntire traces her ancestry in America and England. She learned some very painful truths, including one about a relative who was a slave owner. That fact bothered her, but she faced it with grace.

Then she learned she had a relative involved in a lesser known side of the servitude issue in America. Reba was incensed that the father of a nine-year-old boy would sell his son as an indentured servant and send him off to America. Reba felt the father had abandoned his son. Through the research of a genealogist, she learned the more likely reason why the child's father would send the young boy on a dangerous voyage alone, to work as essentially a slave. Her heart completely broke. The emotions of anger melted into love and gratitude. You'll have to watch the episode to find out why.

In Reba's show and every other episode, *Who Do You Think You Are?* follows an individual through the discovery of very real, very personal stories using old photos and documents, and knowledge from various experts around the world. As the featured star encounters each discovery, they experience a broad range of emotion and see a variety of odd coincidences. When their discovery wraps up at the end of the episode, they've learned a lot and have something to share with their children and grandchildren and often a desire to learn more. Sometimes, they have a desire to change or continue on the legacy they learned. Not every story is happy, but every story is real.

When examining other entertainment media, a few key elements are necessary to please an audience. A successful television show, movie, or book must have a champion, emotion, and a hook. We need someone to cheer for, a story that is engaging, and enough entertainment to keep us tuned in or turning the page. If one of these components is missing, few people will be interested.

Family history is no different. When a person seeks after their legacy (whether to build upon or break free from), they want to know the champions along with the other cast of characters. Some characters we will love. Some we will learn from. And some we might be glad we did not live with because we might not have kept our wits about us in their presence. At the same time, the beloved grandpa may have a dark side. The unpopular uncle may have taught dogs to do tricks. And the ostracized family member might have influenced the world for good, despite the black sheep status.

Real people are not one dimensional but have multiple facets to their lives. All of these family members taken in context with their struggles, triumphs, defeats, heartaches, and strengths provide a range of emotions. You will scream. You will sorrow. You will celebrate. You can understand, or you may never comprehend. Regardless, you will find enough emotion, when you do your research well, to keep you hooked. The quest to know. The quest to learn. The quest to share. The quest to forgive. The quest to honor. Your hook, based on the emotion caused by the champions (or scoundrels) are the core of family history done well.

Family History

Did you ever stop to realize that Family History has the word 'story' in it? Family history is the stories of families. When we forget stories, the work of research and the sharing of our discoveries becomes boring... just like an unsuccessful TV show.

Let's emphasize this another way. When someone says, "I'm going to do my family history or genealogy," they usually mean filling in pedigree charts and family group sheets. Additionally, most every beginning family history class will show you a pedigree chart and tell you to start filling it out. If you wanted to earn the Boy Scouts of America Genealogy

15

Merit Badge, six of the ten required assignments deal with charts and resources and four deal with stories. However, Family History is not pedigree charts and group sheets.

Family History

Family history is not a collection of pedigree charts bound in Books of Remembrance. Family History is not ahnentafel descendant reports bound between leather covers. Family history is something much richer and deeper than what appears on charts.

Charts visually organize relationships. They are tools much the same as a graphic organizer or an outline helps you write a creative story or an essay when you were in school.

When you reimagine your definition of 'Family History' to include a broader scope, you'll realize a fact supports a story but not the entirety of it.

Family history is not this:

Lewis S Brown
1918 - 1978

or this:

Lewis Sherman Brown

b. 18 Sep 1918 in Columbus, Franklin, Ohio
d. 18 Sep 1978 in Columbus, Franklin, Ohio

or even this:

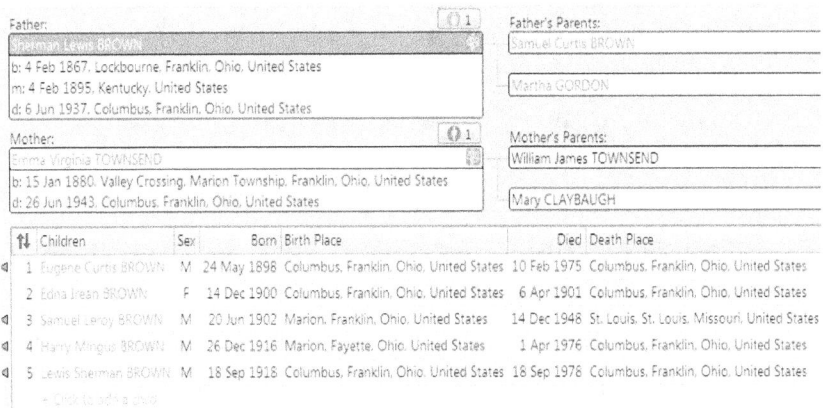

Looking at these facts, do you know much about Lewis Brown?

If you focus on completing a pedigree chart, you'll likely stop there. Sure you might need a few documents to find the correct dates, but other than that, your purpose was to complete a chart. Once the chart is complete, your task is done. Sadly, few of your family members will care.

On the other hand, family history focuses on the stories of Lewis.

> **Family history** is that Lewis Brown has three daughters who fondly remember dancing with him. It is my yearning for this experience as he died when I was a little girl.

> **Family history is** that Lewis Brown was an assistant bowling manager for Swan Lanes in Columbus, Ohio. He participated in numerous tournaments. He earned several prizes, including a

silver tea set. Family history is the question of whether he ever bowled a 300 game. Two of his daughters remember differently.

Family history is that Lewis Brown was a home delivery milkman for Borden's. When he wasn't driving his route, he would usher football games at the Ohio State University stadium. When his delivery route changed and required working during home games, Lew would listen to the Buckeyes on the truck radio while making deliveries. Family history is the fact that one of his granddaughters would rather have gone to the rival University of Michigan before attending Ohio State.

Family history is that Lewis Brown served in the Army during World War II. His wife was left behind to care for his ailing mother. It is the fact that Lewis returned home, perhaps without permission, to see his new baby girl before traveling overseas to India. Family history is the fact that his children and grandchildren loved his military photo because his eyes seem to follow you around the room.

Family history is that Lewis Brown died on his birthday at the age of 60. He left behind a wife, one daughter still in high school, and two married daughters with five grandchildren between them. It's the fact that he died due to esophageal cancer caused by smoking. Family history is the fact that his entire family dearly missed him.

Family history is every story, every artifact, and all the memories that are found between the birth and death dates. No vital record you can find will tell the things I just shared, but they do contribute to who Lewis Sherman Brown is.

1918 — 1978

My journey through family history began with my Grandma Helen's photos on her walls, and her desire to tell me all the stories of the people she loved. Sadly, I was young and had not given much thought to the fact that she would not be alive forever. She passed away during my teen years, and those stories died with her. I have spent years trying to regather her photo collection and some of the stories she shared. It would have been so much easier if I had taken the time when she was alive to record her stories. I do not want this to happen to anyone else.

As you work on your family research, remember that people and their stories matter. The facts will turn up when you focus on the heart of family history, the story. And when you concentrate on the heart of the matter, you will find it difficult to stop working on your family history.

Discover

Knowing that family history is your family plus their stories, let's discover the people that make up our family trees. Let's say you have a school assignment to write a report about one of your ancestors, alive or deceased. Where would you start to learn about this person?

Perhaps the person is still alive, and you can just talk to them. You could call or visit in person. If you visit in person, you'd ask to see photos and mementos that tell about their life. A baseball player may have trophies and sports possessions to share. A military vet may have various items related to his or her service. A talented artist may have knitting, tatting, painting, or other handiwork to show you. Perhaps the relative was a part of a motorcycle gang or fraternal club and saved mementos from his or her involvement. Your living ancestor may have photo albums filled with memories you can then discuss. The possibilities are endless once you begin focusing on a living person.

If your ancestor is deceased, you would probably start by looking at what has already been written about or created by the person. If you happen to have a famous ancestor, you could do an internet search to find what already exists about him or her. Most likely, your relative is not so famous and little is available on the internet. So, where are you going to turn for more information?

If you're lucky, you have a genealogist in the family, and you could contact that person. They will overwhelm you with documents, charts, and hopefully stories. If you're super lucky, someone has written a book with your ancestor's life story, or perhaps that ancestor kept a journal.

If you're starting from scratch and your ancestor is deceased, are you out of luck? Should you just give up? Of course not. You can discover their stories in much the same way you would using a family historian or talking to the living relative. You would turn to their photos, their possessions, and people who knew them.

 **Family history research begins with photos, possessions, and people.**

The reason you start with photos, possessions, and people is that you, or your relatives, have easy access to these things. As you start examining these resources, you may find more than you think you had, or much less. Regardless, search through these sources for the 'dash between the date' information. Look for a deeper understanding of the individuals you call family.

Photos

Imagine finding a photo series with your mother at the welcome home event for your Dad's cousin after he completed his service in the Vietnam War. There is no photo of your Dad. In the collection of photos, you see the cousin's sister, his mother, your mother, and your brother as a baby. While examining the entire set of photos from this event, you may notice that one of the adults was behind the camera since no photo has all of the adults present at the homecoming. What else can you discover from these photos? If you can't make a determination, what questions could you ask your father's aunt, his cousins, or your mother about the occasion? What can you ask your father about why he wasn't there to greet his cousin but your mother, his wife, was?

That's what discovery is. Discover things in your photos that prompt more questions or provide details that you might not have known. You may have known your father's cousin served and survived the Vietnam War. But without the photos, you would not have known who greeted him upon his arrival back in the United States.

Brief Timeline of Photography	
1842 – 1856	Daguerreotype
1855 – 1861	Ambrotype
1860 – 1870	Tintype
1860 – 1880	Carte de Visite
1875 – 1900	Cabinet Card
1900s-	Personal cameras
1900 -	Brownie Box
1913 –	35mm candid cameras
1948 –	Polaroid instant print
1978 –	Konica point & shoot
1986 –	Fuji Single Use Camera
2000 –	Camera phones

 # Photos provide a wealth of information.

Photos can provide a wealth of information. Look through the photo collections you and your family members have. Some photos will be carefully preserved and properly labeled. They will provide names, dates, and occasions. From this information, you can start to see a story develop.

Some photos do not have all the facts recorded on them. If you're lucky, you have a living relative who can identify an unlabeled person or event. Or, perhaps you have a collection of photos that are labeled which can assist you in determining who is in a photo. Even if you only have sketchy information about a photo, there is still much you can learn from photos.

Look at the following photo. What can you learn about the person from this photo?

Notice what the woman is wearing. Notice where she is. Notice the objects in the photo. You can determine that this woman probably was not wealthy given her clothing and hair style. You can roughly date the photo based upon the coloration of the

photo and by the paper type (if you were holding it in your hand). You could also date the photo by the water pump that is in the yard. You can see how close the homes are in the photo. What other details are overlooked?

As you can see, there are a lot of details you can learn from a photo. I am fortunate enough to know that this person was Evaline (Townley) Peak. I didn't know much about the life of Evaline Peak, but now I have discovered some clues about her and her lifestyle. Plus, having a face to put with a name on my family tree is such a treat.

You can learn similar things with your collection of photos, labeled or not. Pay attention to the people in the photos. Photos reveal their relationships to one another, their socioeconomic status, their occupations, their interests, their physical attributes, their lifestyle, their homes, their businesses, and more. The details within a photo, as well as the processing of the photo, can help you date the photo. Dating the photo can help you learn more information about your ancestors as well.

Photos are only as good as what you have access to and what was preserved. Before about 1840, you won't find photos of your ancestors (although for wealthier ancestors, there may be painted portraits). For the photos you do have, you can see the vast information they hold. The more information you have connected with your photos, the easier it is to build your family history later.

As you look at the photos of your family members, you may not only discover stories and clues, but you may also notice the condition of the photos. You may either feel great sorrow for how poorly the photos are preserved, frustrated that the collection was not better labeled, or sing praises for the person who cared for these great resources.

Review your photo collection and consider the following things:

Are my photos labeled?

Are they organized and properly preserved?

Do I know the stories about the photos?

Can I ask someone more about the photos?

Can I make conclusions based on the clues in the photos?

Many resources are available to care for our family photo collections. Discover what has been done and still needs to be done to care for these priceless items so that the 22nd Century can enjoy them. If you are looking to make a huge impact in family history, you can make that impact by caring for the family photo collection.

If your photos need labeling, that's your first priority. If the collection is unorganized, that is your urgent project. If the photos are not stored properly, research and acquire the proper storage solutions. If all you ever did was preserve and organize your family's photo collection, you would be doing more family history than 99% of the world population.

Possessions

When genealogists mention sources for our ancestors, they usually mean birth, marriage, and death records. Paperwork is great, but that's not the only evidence worth examining. Most vital records document only that we existed. Looking at our ancestor's possessions provides clues to our ancestor's character or may bring some family legends to light.

Notice this medal. What can you discover about it? It's a military cross that has something to do with rifles. Simple enough. Having an artifact like this can help you know where to look for more information. This medal belonged to my Grandpa Lew Brown (the one mentioned earlier). I know that he lived between 1918 and 1978. I know that he served in World War II and this

What can you tell about the person who owned this medal?

medal was with a collection of other items associated with his service. Knowing the context behind an object can also help you identify the who and the what of an object.

World War II buffs will know that this is a United States Army Marksmanship Qualification Badge. The cross indicates the individual qualified at the first of three certifications called "Marksman." The two additional ranks are "Sharpshooter" and "Expert." The tags suspended from the cross are Army Weapon Qualification Clasps that indicate which weapons the soldier was qualified as a marksman to use, in this case, a small caliber pistol and a rifle. If you did not know all of this information, you could ask someone who knows or use the internet to do a quick search.

What can you discover about a woman who owned this pin? With three different colored gems, one could guess that this was a piece given to a mother to symbolize her children. You may infer that the mother had three children, as there are three gem colors, the others are 'plain' diamonds. The gems were purple, green, and blue. You could assume the order of the colors signifies the order of the children and their corresponding birth months. If you didn't know birth months for a set of children, this pin can help you solve a mystery.

What can you tell about the person who owned this pin?

Next, do you know if this was a gift or a self-purchased item? The answer could reveal much about the individual as a mother and her relationship with her children. Do you know how often the mother wore this pin? The answers will uncover clues to her appreciation for the pin and the children it represents.

What can you learn about the person who owned the next pictured possession? You may recognize this item and it's connection with the Girl Scouts of America organization. You might know that green felt is the adult insignia tab that could hold the other insignia. You might also recognize that the felt material has been replaced by a ribbon-like fabric. This fact may help you determine a date when the leader was

What can you learn from this item?

involved in the organization. Those familiar with the organization should recognize the World Trefoil Pin, the yellow bar signifying the adult position pin, the membership pin, and finally the Membership Numeral Guard. Who owned this pin? A woman with a desire to help children, either her own or others in her community.

If you wanted to learn more about what things a leader would have done and what the specific insignia mean, you could ask a current Girl Scout leader, a former Girl Scout leader, or again use the internet. The things you learn can help you better understand the volunteer work the owner of the insignia did.

Review your ancestors possessions in the same fashion as you did their photos. You will discover little puzzle pieces about their life. Depending on what is in your collection, you may discover interests, faith, employment, skills, personality, and heritage. Once you have explored the stories awaiting hidden in your personal collection, you can investigate the collections your living relatives possess.

Many times, possessions will only give you a small glimpse into an individual. Some artifacts give you more details than others, but each one can deepen and enrich the stories of your family members. It is sad that these items are often overlooked. All too soon, the stories are forgotten.

I have one friend who has an antique cabinet that belonged to a great-ancestor. The friend doesn't know which ancestor on which side of the family the cabinet belonged to. The story about the cabinet is lost. However, "it's a family heirloom, so I keep it" is such a tragic state of the memories. Another friend has an attic full of possessions that has been collecting since the home was built in the mid-1800s. Few people go into the attic, and few people know all that the attic holds. The stories behind the possessions are slowly slipping from memory. If the house ever leaves the family, the stories may be forgotten and the items discarded without care. Learn the stories behind the artifacts, large and small, that belonged to your family.

A quick word of caution. Having an artifact doesn't mean you have the full story. You need to dig deeper to understand the item's full significance.

You might recognize this jacket as belonging to

What is the deeper story for this jacket?

someone in high school. Look closely. Do you recognize the clubs and organizations this person participated in? A closer examination will reveal the year the owner graduated high school. If you didn't know which high school the owner graduated from, you can use the letters and check for the high schools in the area your ancestor resided to discover the name of their alma mater. The jacket provides many details and can help you discover hidden facts, but that's not the full story.

Notice the kind of material that the sleeves are made of. It is a stiff, leather-like fabric. If you can imagine how thick this fabric is and you know something about sewing, then you can imagine

One deeper story involves the person who sewed on these patches.

how difficult it would be to sew on this fabric. A sewing machine can't easily reach into the sleeves to attach the patches without sewing the sleeves closed.

These patches were all hand sewn by a mother who was proud of her daughter. That's a sweet story, but it goes deeper. I told my mother, who had calloused and bleeding fingers, to stop sewing these patches on my sleeves. It wasn't worth the pain. Just pick a few and be done. My stubborn mother said, "If you earned a patch, it was going on the jacket!" Don't say I didn't try to stop her.

Be advised there is another warning with possession,s since they can not talk. Just as there are deeper stories below the surface of the possessions, some items are misleading.

Imagine for a moment you find this watch face in your family collection. Inscribed on the back is the phrase "For my dearest Mary." The watch belongs to a Grandpa Kevern. You know that Grandpa had no relative named Mary. Before you jump to the conclusion that Grandpa Kevern was a philanderer, you have to know another thing about him.

The inscription of the back of this watch is misleading.

Grandpa Kevern would walk the streets of downtown Salt Lake City in the early morning hours for his daily exercise. He would dress in a ratty, old coat and he looked very much like a homeless person. He had been stopped on occasion and offered money by caring individuals wanting to help, not knowing that he was very frugal and had plenty of money saved away for the rest of his life. When he tried to tell them all he was doing was exercising, the kindhearted individuals were confused and hurt he wouldn't let them 'help.' During his daily walks, Grandpa would find change and jewelry on the streets with no way of returning the objects, so he kept them. Some were re-purposed for his wife and daughters. Others were placed into boxes of collected junk. Over several years, he gathered enough money and valuables to take his wife on a trip to Hawaii and other vacations.

Knowing the story of Grandpa Kevern's daily walks and his finds on those walks, you would hesitate to label him as a philander when you find a watch with a 'strange' inscription on it. We may feel sorry that the watch was not returned to the beloved Mary, yet we'd love having an odd piece to remember Grandpa Kevern.

Review your family treasures and consider the following things:

Are my items labeled?

Are they organized and properly preserved?

Do I know the stories about the possessions?

Can I ask someone more about the possessions?

Can I make conclusions about the possessions?

As you have searched through your ancestors' possessions, you may come across documents and writings of your ancestors. You may find a family Bible, journals, personal histories, life event records, school records, fraternal organization papers, military service documents, wills, obituaries, and paper records that make a genealogist's heart sing. Look for documents that support the possessions that you find. My Grandpa Lew had saved not only a few of his medals from World War II but also his discharge papers and service maps. Combining these papers with his medals and photos from his service, I now have a deeper understanding of Grandpa Lew for my family to learn and remember.

Mementos and heirlooms have many wonderful stories to share. Paper documents add further stories or may provide the facts for the stories behind the artifacts.

You will discover many excellent stories about your ancestors as you look to their possessions and papers. Make this investigation an important part of your research.

People

People have a lot of stories to tell that make them 'more real' to their children and grandchildren. Photos, documents, and writings often support their stories. Some stories have no accompanying photos or artifacts. The best way to learn stories involves talking to your relatives.

My children love to hear about how I have trouble sharing brownies. Seriously, brownies are an addiction for me. As a newlywed, I made a batch of brownies for my darling husband and me. In an effort to turn over a new leaf and share, I divided the dessert in half, evenly too. After eating my half in less than a day, I noticed my husband didn't have the same weakness. Meaning, he had only eaten one brownie from his half. Hmm.... odd. When you make brownies, they are supposed to be eaten. The next day, I was craving brownies, but mine were all gone. On Andy's plate, only one more small piece of his half was eaten. Very, very odd. Thinking he would never be able to eat the brownies before they went bad, I decided to eat a portion. I was only thinking of him! Who wants to eat stale brownies? Unfortunately, after another day and Andy only taking one more small part of his half, I just had to help him out. I finished off the whole plate.

Since those early days, I've changed my ways. I am no longer a brownie thief. These days, the kids know that I'll share on the first day but there are no promises we'll have any brownies on day two. As my children grow and have children of their own, if I don't record my brownie addiction, it will be lost.

Additionally, my kids also love my misadventures in cooking. Such as forgetting to put eggs in brownies when guests were over. (I still can't believe I ruined my favorite dessert.) Or the time I asked for paprika instead of cinnamon on cottage cheese and pineapples. I tend to misspeak a lot - like Doc in *Snow White and the Seven Dwarfs* - but my darling thought I was having a pregnant moment. Nope, just a brain hiccup. I was convinced I said cinnamon, not paprika, even though he repeated back to me what I said. I was adamant; I wanted paprika. One tastes great on a treat, the other not so much. Many families have recipes to pass down from their mothers and grandmothers. It's a great treasure. For my children, they'll have stories of my misadventures in the kitchen!

Take the time to interview people, even if you have something your relative wrote. My darling Grannie Brown was given a personal history book with a variety of questions to fill out. She was given plenty of lines to write her story. Let's just say that 75% of the book was never completed. And when she did write something, it was painfully brief.

When looking through the book after her funeral, my cousins and I were at first surprised at how little Grannie wrote. But then my cousins insisted, "That's Grannie!" Had I known about this book while Grannie was alive and how short her answers were, I would have taken pains to ask for more details. Thankfully, my aunt had video recorded some of the questions.

I miss my Grannie, and I'd like to have more details. I'd like more stories about her sister, her mother, her father, and her grandparents. I'd love to have more stories about her life when Grandpa Lew went overseas. I'd love to know more about her work at the Xerox Company. I would love to have the story written down about how she sent my Navy pilot cousin a plunger as a going away gift. The list goes on and on. Take time to talk to people who are alive. And if they have passed on, ask your aunts, uncles, cousins, nephews, and other family members and the ancestor's friends to tell you more. You will discover wonderful stories.

You may also find some tragic ones. Perhaps an ancestor was an alcoholic and destroyed their family. Perhaps your female ancestor had multiple miscarriages or an illegitimate child. Maybe your ancestor abandoned their family or was imprisoned. The show *Who Do You Think You Are?* has shared examples of people many descendants would like to forget. Black sheep are in every family; however, even celebrities have realized there is power in knowing the good and the bad, so that we can better cope with the present and bless future generations.

Don't be afraid to go where the pain is. You'll be surprised what knowledge you can receive by seeing the highs and lows on your family tree. Don't be ashamed of your ancestors. They are not you. It is what it is and what you and your family does with the knowledge will be judged, not who is in your bloodline.

Review your journals, letters, and interviews, then consider the following things:

Do I know who is speaking?

Do I know who or what they are talking about?

Did I forget to record an important story or memory?

Can I ask someone to tell me more stories?

Can I make conclusions about the stories already recorded?

If you have no written or recorded family history, make recordings of your relatives or record your memories of the ancestors you knew. Conduct written, audio, or video interviews. Preserve the perishable before it's too late. Don't depend on someone to always remember or be around to tell the stories.

Family History
Discoveries

Are found in your home!

As you can see, family history starts at your home. It can be done by anyone and doesn't require special training. You now know what the hidden treasures look like and can assess what is missing in your collection. Make plans to preserve your discoveries you currently have and will obtain in the future.

As you start in your home with the photos, possessions, and people, you find the heart of family history and start wanting to learn more about the things you've discovered.

More Discoveries Await

Once you've exhausted your home resources, additional tools can help you find or better understand your family history. These resources expand your family story to fill in the details and give great depth to what you've learned through the photos, possessions, and people.

Your Local Library

Books have been written about all sorts of events that happened during the life of your ancestors. Find and read books about military campaigns, historical events, natural disasters, political views, and popular trends that your ancestors mention as you reviewed their photos and memorabilia or spoke with them. Perhaps you are not familiar with the locations mentioned in your ancestors' lives. Your library may have local and state histories to help you discover what your ancestor's hometown was like. Additionally, you may discover books about the particular occupation, heritage, immigration, and interests of your ancestor. Discoveries await you and your local librarian will be happy to assist you in finding books in their collection.

On-line Research Websites and Family Trees

I'll briefly mention online family trees which assist with in-depth research. However, investigate online trees for the photos and stories that people have linked to your common trees. My husband visited FamilySearch.org and searched the Family Tree for an ancestor. He discovered a photo he'd never seen. It showed a museum display piece containing artifacts that once belonged to the ancestor in question. He could see a photo of the possessions of his ancestor and thus learn more about the individual.

Some submissions to these websites have included family Bible pages, stories about land purchases, funeral programs, and the like. There is no guarantee something new will be available. You never know what you'll discover on these websites until you search.

While you're discovering photos and stories, you may also find documents linked to your ancestor's profiles. These records help you know more about your ancestor's life and give clues for further research. Leave the further until after you read Chapter 3: Organize. For now, focus on discovering the story of your ancestor.

Wikipedia

If you haven't discovered *Wikipedia: The Free Encyclopedia*, you're missing out on an easily accessible wealth of knowledge. Remember the days of using an encyclopedia to look up information for school reports? In the 21st century, we don't need to consult out-of-date encyclopedias when we can access reasonably up-to-date entries in an online encyclopedia, Wikipedia.org.

Let's say you don't know much about the history of Bryan, Texas and you live in Iowa. The local library doesn't have much information on the particular location but has a general history book about Texas. However, Wikipedia will reveal who founded the city and why it bears that name. Additionally, the site entry information probably includes historical population numbers for Bryan so you can determine how large the city was when your ancestor lived there. As you learn more about the city, you can add greater depth to the sights and place they called home.

You could also research things such as the military medal I mentioned before and various organizations your relatives participated in (Girl Scouts, Shriners, Marine Corps, etc.). The information you find on Wikipedia articles is created in collaboration with others. You can find detailed information, supported by many sources, and written in an informative and neutral view. As such, this information is often as accurate as you may find in a printed encyclopedia. (In fact, studies have shown that the Wikipedia entries are just as accurate as printed encyclopedias - so much so that many printed encyclopedias are no longer in business).

Google, Bing, Other Search Engines

Search engines are great in the discovery phase. You could type in your ancestor's name and hope you get lucky, although this approach generally doesn't generate much success. For the most part, the information I find on a specific individual is in an online database. Most search engines are not designed to collect links for you from databases.

However, you can have a lot of success searching for more information about the things you want to better understand in the discovery phase. For instance, my Great Grandfather William James Townsend (or Townson) fought in the American Civil War. I found his unit number and was able to search that term with Google, "Civil War OH Infantry Co. K 133rd Regt." The search results included websites that shared details about the unit's campaigns and the leaders. With this information, I discovered a deeper knowledge of William's involvement and a likely brother in the same unit!

Perhaps you discovered that your grandfather emigrated to the United States on the *RMS Olympic*. Your search engine should not only have links to Wikipedia but also may find links to other pages and images of this ship. You will learn the *Olympic* was a sister ship to the *Titanic* and operated before and after the *Titanic* sailed. Not only can you learn about this ship itself, but you can also search for the weather at the time of your ancestor's crossing, the cost of a ticket, what meals were served in various classes, and much, much more.

I have only scratched the surface of resources available to help you discover your family's stories outside of your home. By investigating what you have easy access to, you will learn a wealth of information. Then you can keep the discovery process going.

 Start Simple

Too often beginning family historians are told to build a tree and start searching for documents to prove facts they know. How absolutely tragic it is to start from this perspective. Time and time again, new genealogists don't know enough information to complete a four generation pedigree chart. In fact, many times people don't know their grandmother's maiden name or the birth dates and places of any grandparents. Sometimes, they know little about their parents. But everyone has heard a story about someone they call family.

Start by discovering who your ancestors are with what is readily available in your home and in the heads of your relatives. Search to understand and discover their stories, and you will be rewarded with facts during the process.

Deepen your understanding of who your families are until you can tell someone else your ancestor's story, focusing on their character (for good or ill), the emotional connection (or disconnect) you feel, and the reason why they are interesting (their hook).

As you focus your efforts on your family members and their stories, you may fall in love with family history. You won't necessarily like every aspect of this hobby, but find things you enjoy. Ultimately, you assist others in your family not only to know their history, but help them in their search as well.

Organize

Throughout the discovery phase of family history, you have learned new things, gathered information, and noted needs to care for family treasures. You have opened your heart toward the stories of family. You have started in the right place. As you discover your hidden family treasures in photos, possessions, and people, a yearning arises for what you want to do with this newly discovered information. Surely what you uncovered should be shared with others so they don't have to retrace your steps. Instead, leave a trail for others to go further than where you'll eventually stop. Before climbing your tree to higher branches, begin with the end in mind. Then develop a plan to organize your discoveries and future research to achieve that end goal.

Know Your Goals

Stop and answer this question: **What is your why?**

Before you take another genealogy class or look up another document, establish your goals. Knowing your goals determine the rest of your family history journey.

Don't worry if your goal seems trivial or silly. People participate in genealogy for a large variety of reasons. The only reason that matters is yours. What is your why?

Is your why listed below?

Reasons People Do Genealogy

- Curiosity
- Gain admittance into fraternal organizations
- Gain admittance into historical lineage-based societies
- Write a biographical sketch or eulogy
- Complete school assignments
- Preserve your family history for future generations
- Downsize a home before a more or after a death
- Share stories at a family reunion
- Write entries for county histories
- Prove a family legend true
- Understand your heritage
- Earn a Boy Scout Merit Badge
- Cope with a legacy of family abuse and neglect
- Take names to a temple
- Find biological relations
- Prepare donations for a museum
- Research a person for a reenactment

Once you know your why, you can develop an organization system around that goal. Let's examine a few goals and how they direct the next phase of involvement

Curiosity

Suppose you have seen the Ancestry.com commercials that suggest that "You don't need to know what you're looking for, you just need to look." Perhaps *Genealogy Roadshow*'s problem solving for non-celebrities piqued your interest. No matter the trigger, you're curious and we should celebrate. When you do genealogy, you'll poke around, looking for something and hopefully find enough to satisfy that wonder. In-depth is of no value to you at this point. Perhaps in the future, but methodical research will spoil your interests.

A curious family historian needs a flexible organization system to accommodate their discoveries as they stumble upon them. The system should be very simple, such as a folder of family history discoveries for a few individuals. Curiosity may turn into a passion or can be transferred to other researchers. As such, the curious researcher should keep a record of where discoveries were found and develop a system to preserve any discoveries along the way.

The goal of curiosity being the guide requires a simple organization plan that can expand as needed.

Proving Lineage

Proving lineage to join a society, such as Daughters of the American Revolution, requires thorough research. The focus of such research is documentation and analysis. The records that matter are those that determine biological relationships with little emphasis of the story behind the individuals on those records. Hopefully, you'll learn amazing stories along the way, so that you have interesting stories to share about your relatives when your research is accepted by the organizations.

You are not just joining to join but to share and learn more as well.

A lineage-based family historian needs a strict organization system that checks off the necessary requirements for application approval. The system should be broader than a curious researcher but confined to only direct ancestors. A lineage seeking researcher would do well to include a system for preserving the discoveries about their ancestors. The system could be an additional folder or binder section within the strict system required for pedigree proving genealogy.

The goal of proving lineage requires a structured organization plan which benefits from a story repository addendum.

Biographical Sketch

Biographical researchers accumulate stories and documents about one person. Research may extend to immediate family members (parents, spouses, children) as those individuals impact the overall story. Most often, the extended family is researched to the extent relationships are established (John is the son of Bob and Sally).

A biographical research does not need a robust genealogical database to organize numerous family members. A sketch writer needs a plan to manage the stories and documents of the focus of the biography.

The goal of biographical sketches requires a story and document organization for one person.

Preservation focused family historians or individuals disposing of an estate need a quick way to shift through and digitize photos, possessions, and papers to ensure legacies are passed down to future generations.

Once items are organized and preserved, inheritance issues must be resolved and the easiest method of passing along legacy is a physical product (a book, scrapbook or other format) or a sharing site for other researchers and family members to access. Research and source citations are of little importance to a preservation and downsizing historian.

The goal of preservation and downsizing is rapidly organizing and sharing discoveries with others.

Goals Determine Organization

Did you notice how the goals dictated the kind of organization system each research needs? Consider the other reason why individuals research and what type of organization system they'll need to preserve their recent discoveries and compile future insights as they come to light. The pattern is the same. Goals determine organization, so begin with the end in mind.

Give serious thought about what you want to accomplish. Just like there is no one right way to organize your research, there is no one right reason to be involved in family history. Truly determine what you hope to accomplish and let that be your guide.

Goal-oriented Questions to Determine Your Tasks

- Do I start building a tree?

- Do I go looking for vital documents?

- Do I start interviewing for further information?

- Can I start writing what I've already learned?

- Do I need to purchase appropriate storage boxes for my albums and possessions?

- Do I need to interview someone to learn the stories behind the photos, the possessions, or the people?

- Is there more to be learned about life as a rural immigrant farmer in Johnson County, Iowa?

As you recognize your goals and what you want to accomplish in your genealogical quest, you can quickly determine what needs to be done next. Start by asking yourself targeted, goal-oriented questions.

Did you see your next step on the list? Notice how knowing where you want to go determines the next steps in the process. Although the list is brief, recognize the steps that you may take now or in the future. You may also think of your own. Write them in the margins of the books so you'll remember the possibilities.

 # Goals determine organization and your tasks in family history.

Let's suppose you have an ancestor who served in a particular unit in the American Civil War but was honorably discharged because of a stated condition "erysipelas." You don't know much about this illness that afflicted your ancestor. Your next step would be to investigate the illness and how it might have been treated during the Civil War.

Your next steps would be to create a To-Do list with the following tasks:

- Find out what "erysipelas" is and how it was treated during the 1860s.

- Determine if my relative was entitled to a veteran's pension because of his illness.

- Determine if my relative received a pension.

- Review the Civil War Pension file for any additional discoveries about my ancestor and his illness.

Once answers to these questions come in, how I file them will be determined based upon my goals. If I am curious and working on a biographical sketch, I will have a file that focuses on my ancestors Civil War service and include the documentation and explanations supporting his service and erysipelas. If I'm a more strict researcher, I would create folders, source citations, conclusions, and written summaries about my discoveries and file them. The pension file would likely go into a common folder of all Civil War pension files or with the actual ancestor named in the pension.

The Point You Get to Stop

Selecting your goals now helps you define a clear stopping point! There is always something more that can be discovered, researched, preserved, recorded, and shared. Genealogy is fun but life often interferes with family history. Deciding upon a goal gives you a clear stopping point.

Perhaps you have inherited your parents home and suddenly need to clean out 40 years worth of stuff but don't want to lose your heritage as you do so. You're stopping point is when everything is sorted, organized, preserved, and digital files or physical possessions are shared. No further research for you.

Perhaps you want to begin to participate in family history but have limited experience. Your goal could be to organize, preserve, or research something online each Monday for 30 minutes. You add to your organization system a little at a time but stop when the timer beeps.

Beginning with the end in mind eliminates guilt. With a defined goal, you stop when you reach that goal and know you've added to the family history body of knowledge.

Do not be surprised if you complete your goal, and decide to start another project. Family history can be very addicting. If you complete one goal and enjoy it so much that you want to start another, follow this system to create and accomplish your new goal. If you complete that goal and you're no longer interested, you can stop and be satisfied

If everyone did a little something to preserve their own family's history and heritage, then family history would be a lot easier to compile. Do your part, whatever that may be, no matter how small. Set your goals so you know when to stop and feel a sense of accomplishment.

Organizing Options

With your goals determining your organization, review some of the systems family historians have used to manage their materials. There is no one right way to organize your files and information. Few genealogists agree on the one right way to organize documents, photos, and possessions. Avoid the quest for the one perfect organizational plan.

Your organizational goal is to find the items you want when you want them. If your system accomplishes this, then it's the right system for you.

Avoid the pressure to organize, or reorganize, everything at once. Organize as you go. When you make a discovery, determine where the discovery should be filed and then place it there. You do not have to look at a stack of papers, research, photos, and such, and feel like everything has to be organized at once. Develop your system as you slowly work through your discoveries. That way, if you need to make any changes, you make them while your system is still flexible enough to accommodate any modifications.

Entire websites and books are written about each of the following methods. Each method can be easily adapted to paper storage or electronic filing systems.

The extreme example of the Organize By Family system is one folder per family consisting of a father, mother, and their children. Information in this folder includes the genealogy charts specific to this family, vital records about the family members, photos, stories, journals, research notes, etc.

Remember that the parents are children in other families and their information would need to be copied and placed in the folders of their respective parental households. Additionally, many of the children will form their families after marriage. The documents in the parental family file folder will need to be copied into folders where the child becomes a spouse/parent.

Some suggest that you keep a log in your files that indicate that additional source items are in a particular file. This method would allow you to place all the elements about a person before marriage in the file folder of their parents. Any item about life after marriage would be placed in the folder of marriage. Then create a log stating that a married person's birth certificate is located in the parental file folder. And, the death certificate would be made mention of in the parental file folder but placed in the folder where the individual was a spouse.

Files are labeled with the husband's name and years. So, if the father of the family was Lewis Brown, the file label would read "BROWN, Lewis 1918-1978." You might even need to add the wife's name, especially if you have multiple ancestors with the same name or if one ancestor married multiple times. For instance, one of my male ancestors had two wives. His first wife would be discussed in the file labeled "SMITH, Andrew N 1855-1933 & Emma Ward." The second wife would be discussed in the folder labeled "SMITH, Andrew N 1855-1933 & Mary Etta Webb."

Organize By Type

The need to make copies of source items to be placed in multiple folders or to keep accurate cross-referencing logs might be cumbersome, some people elect to group their items by type. This system groups all interviews together. All photographs are stored together. All birth certificates with birth certificates, and so on.

Items are identified by the principal individual(s) and ordered alphabetically. So, all the interviewees' recordings are labeled with their name and then filed according to their last name.

Photo albums are grouped by the principal family names and then arranged by surname on a photo album shelf. Loose photos are generally arranged by owner's collection (Aunt Margie's photos or Grandma Maggie's photos) and then ordered by year as much as possible.

There are limitations with this method as well, but the focus is keeping similar type items together with less need to make copies or cross-references.

Having moved numerous times, my organization must be compact and portable so it includes a collection of hard copy and digitized files. I do not make photo copies of anything that is easily accessible online, nor do I download these items to my computer. You won't find census records on my hard drive unless they're downloaded for a current writing project. Online and off, I try to organize my photos by family and then chronologically. I also organize my documents by type and then by principle name. Finally, I use a desktop database to organize my closest relatives. For extended relations, I curate documents and photos using online trees. All of these organization strategies help me keep my genealogy accommodating my needs for portability.

Photo Organization Tips

Chronologically sorted family photo collections help me rapidly create scrapbooks and written family histories. They also help me determine the names of identified individuals.

Organize photos by family but follow these guidelines: a) photos of a person before marriage stays with their parental family; and b) photos after a marriage go into a new family folder. Keep in mind, you don't have to strictly follow these guidelines. In fact, I often will not split off photos of a individual after marriage unless I have 5 or more photos post wedding. Guidelines help you make decisions but they should be adapted to accommodate your needs.

File Folder Tree for Family Photos

Geiszler Family Photos

- Geiszler, Bob Jr & Penny Brown
  - ○ Child of Bob #1 (until married)
  - ○ Child of Bob #2 (until married)
- Geiszler, Bob Sr & Helen Zumstein
  - ○ Geiszler Bob Jr (until he marries Penny Brown)
- Geiszler, George J & Evaline Peak
- Geiszler George B
  - ○ child of George B #1
  - ○ Geiszler Margie
  - ○ child of Margie #1
  - ○ child of Margie #2
  - ○ Geiszler Bob Sr, until he marries Helen Zumstein
- Peak photos (all photos of Peak relatives)
- Zumstein, Robert Victor & Clementine Comfort
  - ○ Child of R. Victor #1
  - ○ Child of R. Victor #2
  - ○ Helen Zumstein until she marries Bob Geiszler Sr

Notice the file folder tree. The heading "Geiszler Family Photos" is a folder. Each bulleted item is a folder under this top level folder. Each sub-point is a sub-folder within the bulleted item's folder. Notice how the Peak folder has no sub-folders. It contains so few photos that breaking it into sub-folders is unnecessary. I create similar folder tree for each grandparent's family lines.

Notice how Margie is a sub-folder for George Geiszler, and she has sub-folders below her name. I have a lot of photos for George and his wife, Evaline. I have many photos of George's children that support a separate folder. George's son married my direct ancestor Helen Zumstein. They formed a family. The photos of Bob Sr. until he married Helen are in the sub-folder under his parents. After he married Helen, those photos are in their joint folder. And so on.

The majority of my photos are in digital form, partly because I have moved often. Additionally, I have scanned many relatives' photo albums when I have visited them and have expanded the family photo archive. I may not have all photos in physical form but I can print them whenever I please.

Digital Photo Naming System

Within the organized file folders appear my sorted images. When viewing the photos, many stories come to life as photos are organized chronologically. As such, strive to name your individual photo files so they can be sorted quickly by filename to manage your files.

Photo Naming Formula

year + month + surname + first name + event + number

Structure file names so you leave clues for the next person who inherits your digital photos. Review the sample files created with the Photo Naming Formula.

> 194109BrownLewisHoneymoon01.jpg
> 194109BrownLewisHoneymoon02.jpg
> 194308BrownLewisWorldWarIIdeploy.jpg
> 1960sBrownPennyTwirling02.jpg
> 196209BrownPennyBridalPortrait01.jpg

The four-digit year is first. Next is a two digit month, if it is known. Penny twirled batons in the 1960s. The exact year and month are unknown, so the year 1960s is used with no month included. Following the month is the surname. You could capitalize the surname if you wish. It's a personal preference. The given name of the person follows their surname. The event in the photo follows the name. Keep it brief and without punctuation. Finally, if multiple photos of the event or person exist, label the photos 01, 02, 03, and so forth. This labeling system helps most programs sort the photos without doing something strange because one name has two digits and another has three.

Document Organization Tips

If you sort your document files by type, all of the same record type for your relatives (no matter if they are ancestors or descendants) are grouped into the document folder. For instance, all the birth certificates are in one folder.

> **Document Naming Formula**
>
> surname + first name + document type + number

When naming your document files, it's easier to look for the key record if the last name of your individual is recorded first on the file and then all of the pertinent details follow. For document type, use an abbreviation such as BC (for birth certificate), MC (marriage record or certificate), etc. Some organizers will add the year of the document. I haven't found the need for this detail. A number is used if there are two or more images in a record set. For instance, a will might span across two pages, and therefore the file name for both pages would be the same except the first would be 01 and the second 02. Here are some file name examples:

BrownLewisBC.jpg

CrowleyJamesBC.jpg
CrowleyJamesJrBC.jpg
CrowleyJaneBC01.jpg
CrowleyJaneBC02.jpg

Continue this process for family Bibles, death certificates, military records, gravestone photos, etc. As a side note, I file photographs of heirlooms and mementos in the photo folders by family name.

 Organize Your Way

Several organization systems claim to be the best for genealogy and family history. While these systems have advantages, the best system is the one where you'll quickly retrieve what you are looking for and is accessible to others if you pass away. Just because my husband can find a tool in the garage in 5 seconds, doesn't mean that space is organized. I can not do the same thing. Organize your files not only to fit your style but to pass on your collections at some future date.

Keep in mind Goals determine organization. A curious person can organize their family archives in the steps above because they're searching for family clues and want to declutter their home. A biographical sketch writer won't need a system as robust. A few folders that divide the life of one individual will suffice. Develop a plan to organize your discoveries. Modify it as needed but stick with a general plan.

Record

When we're excited about the heart of family history, we want to remember all the information we discover and share it with others so that we won't forget it ourselves. With your goals in mind and a method to organize your efforts, record what you have discovered.

Part of recording your findings is preserving what you already have. Preservation is different than organization. Organization dictates where things will be placed for retrieval later. Preservation deals with how you care for your photos, documents, and possessions, so they last for future generations. Organization systems and preservation efforts work together to provide a method for identifying the items and managing their stories

Recording your discoveries can take many forms. You could record in audio or video formats. Creating audio files could be as simple as recording yourself talking into a voice recording app on a smartphone or using a microphone attached to your computer. You could record video using a smartphone, web camera, or a video camera. Not only can you record yourself, but you can also record your living relatives answering questions, telling stories, playing the piano, or singing. The possibilities are only limited by the scope of your vision.

Consider recording your discoveries in written form. Written forms can be longhand, typed, or printed from a computer. Your recordings may be letters, questionnaires, and notes about your discoveries. You could also exchange emails and compile the pertinent information into one file for saving on your computer or for printing out. The writings might also have already been done, such as written compositions by an ancestor like poems, lyrics, essays, or diaries.

 **The format you are most comfortable with is the one that works for you.**

My great aunt Margie started out by writing me letters of family stories and answering questions that I sent her. But being in her eighties, writing became more strenuous on her hands. She had a tape recorder and knew how to use it. She recorded her stories that way. When she filled up a tape, she sent it to me. It worked great.

In contrast, I have come of age during the computer revolution. I don't like to hand write anything. I record my stories using a laptop computer. I type fairly quickly, so I prefer to compose text documents rather than record audio and video of myself. However, I can't type as fast as someone talks. So, if I'm writing my personal history or the discoveries I have made, I type. If I'm working with an ancestor, I record them talking as I ask them questions. Then some day I will transcribe the conversation.

Determine the way that works for you and use it. There's no one right way to record your stories. The only wrong way is to fail to record them at all.

A distinction must be made between recording and sharing. Recording involves taking knowledge and memories from one form and converting them into a usable, non-perishable form. A person's mind is not a usable, non-perishable form but a written letter is. Sharing compiles recordings into a format that is pleasing for a great number of people.

When Aunt Margie recorded her memories, she told stories. Sometimes she was clear and concise. Sometimes she rambled a bit. During the recording phase, what was important is that I captured her stories and the information only she would know. When I share her stories, as discussed in the next chapter, I have to take her stories, along with additional photos, documents, and information and combine that into a comprehensive, and dare I say more enjoyable, book, sound recording, or video.

What Do You Record?

With documents and photos, what you record is easy to pinpoint. You record the pertinent information that the document or photo does not share.

Perhaps you have a **Boy Scouts of America membership card** from the 1930s. In talking with your grandmother, you learned about your grandfather's life-long participation in the organization which isn't recorded on the card.

Perhaps you have an **Eastern Star ring** from your grandmother. Record some of the history of that organization that you found on Wikipedia or using Google Search. Note events the Eastern Star chapter hosted during the years your grandmother was involved with the group. This information was obtained as you searched the internet and found an Eastern Star historian eager to assist you remember the past. You may not know for certain if your grandmother attended the events, but record what was available.

With photos, record the obvious information: names, dates, and places. Be sure to also go deeper. Perhaps there was a funny moment that happened at the event portrayed in the photos. Perhaps you learned some things about your ancestor's personality when talking to living relatives. Perhaps you have a photo of your grandfather playing golf, and you learned what golf course he patronized. Record the golf course's history and amenities during your ancestor's life.

Family stories and information don't always have photos and documents to support them. Stories frequently retold, but have not written down, should be recorded. Record the stories as you remember them or from the person who knows the story (or tells it) best.

During your discovery process, you have probably developed questions that need further researching. Record why further research is necessary.

Did you discover inconsistencies, like stories related to one relative, are attributed to a different person? Record how to associate the proper stories with the correct ancestor.

Did you stumble upon some misinformation that needs to be corrected? Record how relatives can determine which birth date is correct for your adopted aunt.

Did you discover how to keep separate a great-uncle with a fairly common name from others from the town? Record how to keep one Richard Richards separated from another Richard Richards from St. Keverne, England.

Jot down the things you ponder. Through all of your discoveries, organization, and research, your mind may wander and wonder.

Do you wonder how your grandfather dealt with the loss of his father and the remarriage of his mother so soon after his father's death?

Do you wonder how your great grandmother was able to raise 14 children in a two room house in a small rural town?

Do you wonder what the voyage was like for your immigrant family with a husband, wife, and three children under the age of 6?

These reflections may never be resolved through research as they deal with emotions and the details that are not often recorded. These musings are still part of family history. Record them.

Tips on Recording Stories from Photos

Photos should have identification labeled on the back of a photo whenever possible. Many photos in your collection lack any details or enough details for other family members to fully appreciate them. Record the discoveries associated with the photos you have organized.

Label the hard copies

With hard copy photos, use an archival quality pencil or pen to label them. Avoid using ball point pens and strive to only write on the back of photos. If you must write on an image, do not write on the inner part of the photo. Write in the border of a photo.

When you label a photo, keep the information brief. Identifying photos so that someone later knows the basics: name, date, place, occasion.

Names: If all you know is Aunt Ethel, then label your photo, Aunt Ethel. Someone may later figure out who Aunt Ethel is, but they'll have a hard time knowing what Aunt Ethel looks like if you can't leave the clue you do know.

Dates: If you know an approximate date, then write a 'c' and a period before the approximate date (such as c. 1940, this means circa 1940 or about 1940 but the specific year is unknown). Labeling a photo with c. 1940 is much better than nothing at all. If you know the occasion was Easter, but you don't remember the specific date, you could get away with Easter Sunday 1940. Of course, if you know a particular holiday or event, you could look up the specific date in an online calendar.

Do not write so large on the back of original photos that no one else can make corrections or add additional information. Label what you can, but leave room on your photos for more information.

Record and store longer stories

If you have discovered longer stories that complement the photos you have, record that information through audio, video, or written formats. Where you store the recorded stories depends upon your organizational style.

If your organizational style is 'hard copy only,' then write or type the stories that explain the associated photos. Store these writings within the photo storage container. Recognize the stories and photos are likely to be separated in hard copy organization systems should they become disorganized for whatever reason. Make plans to make a project that links the photos and stories together in a more permanent way.

If your photos are in photo albums, number both the album and each page within. In the written story, you can reference the particular photos by album, page number, and then position on the album page. You could store the written stories in the back of the album, in a file folder that contains all similar photo album stories, or even on your computer.

If your organizational style is electronic, you can type the story in a word processing program. Insert photos into the document and save that file with your photo files.

If you make a sound recording, reference the photos either through a numbering system or some other identification method. Then place the sound recording in the folder where the referenced photos are on your computer.

If you make a video recording, be sure to hold up the photos that are discussed as you or your relative shares a story.

Store the hard copies

As you complete your labeling work, ensure that your photo collection is properly preserved for generations to come. Photos were often stored in the following damaging ways:

- **paper clipped together**
- **wrapped in rubber bands**
- **glued in black paper albums that are not acid-free**
- **in magnetic albums with glue strips attach photos to the pages**

If your photos are stored in the above ways, transfer them to a more appropriate storage solution.

Grouping Photos: First and foremost, remove paper clips and rubber bands. To group photos together, use acid-free photo dividers. Label the dividers by family, then by year, month or category to keep them sorted. Store all of these photos in acid-free photo boxes.

Acid-Free Storage: For photos in damaging scrapbooks and albums, remove them when possible without damaging the photos. Before you remove the photos, photograph or scan the arrangement of your photos in an album. The arrangement and notes on these pages can be very important. Then carefully attempt to remove your photos and place them in archival quality photo boxes or photo albums. Most photo albums on the market today are great for preserving your photos, but they can be costly. If cost is a concern, you'll want to consider photo boxes for your small photos and one or two albums for your larger prints.

If you cannot remove the photos from the photo albums without damaging them, leave them in place.

Storing Documents

Storing your documents is similar to how you preserve photos; however, many documents are self-explanatory. For those documents that need an explanation, label your documents on the back side, when possible, using an archival safe pen. Keep your labeling information brief. The advantage to hard copy documents is that you'll generally place these in archival safe file folders or binders. Then make a photocopy of the document and write all of your notes on the photocopy. Store the photocopy with the original document. Now, the recorded discovery stays with the document.

While we're talking about transcribing sound, we should also mention transcribing handwritten documents.

My husband has a family member who wrote letters in a time when paper and postage were very expensive. In the image to the right, you can see how the letters looked. Notice how she would write one-half of the letter from top to bottom, turn the paper a quarter turn and then write on top of that. For most people, this is a novelty but is very, very difficult to read. A transcription makes this novelty understandable.

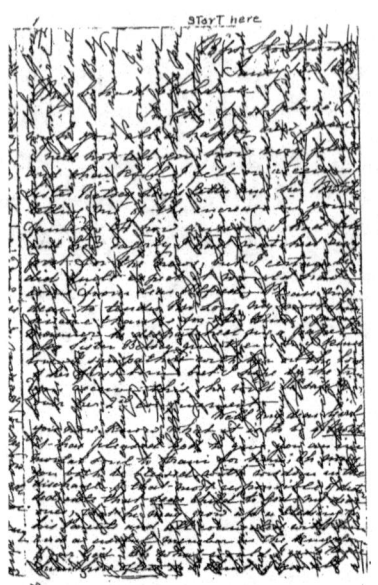

Can you read this? Will your family members be able to?

Don't assume everyone will be able to read cursive handwriting in years to come. Script writing has changed and as time passes the ability to read a certain script becomes more and more difficult. And, dare we mention that some ancestors (or ourselves) had terrible handwriting? A transcription of a letter or handwritten journal can solve this problem. You can add comments to things that someone in future generations might not understand.

Record the Spoken Word

Some people talk better than they write. Sometimes thoughts come to you when you are unable to write, but you can speak a story. That's when audio recordings come in handy.

My Aunt Margie used a tape recorder. She was guided in her recordings by questions that I presented to her. As she answered those questions, she would think of other stories and information and would tell them. It was a painless process for her.

These days, with smartphones, there are many apps that will allow you to record voice. Additionally, you can use a microphone attached to a computer to record sound.

With storage capacities more extensive, you do not need to limit your spoken word recordings to audio only. Smartphone, webcams, and digital video recorders can capture the audio and visual aspects of an interview or musing.

The options for voice or video recordings are more than this book can handle. If you like to make voice recordings, search the internet for tools that can help you accomplish your goals. If you find a tool you might like and are unsure of how to use it, do another internet search for tutorials on the tool you choose.

If you are still uncertain about audio and video recording options, visit your local Family History Center and ask the volunteers there what they might recommend. If your hands are wearing out or you just don't like to write, you do not have to feel that recording your stories is only limited to handwriting or typing.

Capturing the voice of someone is awesome, but preserving it for future generations can be difficult as recording formats change. Do you have a record player at home? Do you have a cassette player? Do you have the ability to play reel to reel films? Do you still have a VHS player? Since the 1980s, a variety of recording formats have come into existence, replaced older technology, and have been replaced with newer technology.

Knowing that formats change, transcribe any video or audio recording you make or have. The transcription will survive audio/video technology changes. Additionally, a transcription of a recording is easier to include in other formats, such as a book. If you should ever misplace an audio or video recording, you have a backup of the stories in the transcription.

Another advantage of transcribing audio records is overcoming the flaws inherent in everyday creations. Unless you have access to a professional recording studio, you may encounter some problems. It's frustrating to listen to a recording when a car passes by as someone tells the punchline of a joke. A microphone can pick up the sounds of the machines common in homes, like air conditioners and refrigerators, that people tend to tune out in everyday life. Additional distractions can enter into a recording, which can be overcome to an extent by a transcription. You wouldn't want to lose that punchline forever because of the limitations of your recording.

Transcriptions also allow you to add commentary to what was spoken but not elaborated on in the audio recording. For instance, perhaps your relative mentions a person's name but does not tell who they are. With your notes, you could identify who that person was. You can clarify nicknames for people, places, and activities. You can explain relationships that are not clear. You can add details that will help explain things future generations might not have knowledge of, such as what a Buster Brown haircut is.

 Record Your Discoveries As You Go.

To sum up, after you make discoveries in your family history with photos, possessions and people, record what you've discovered. When you have everything you've discovered recorded, you can share what you've learned.

In 2011, I took a research trip to Ohio to meet relatives, access archives, and discover many new to me photos and stories. In 2012, my grandmother and mother passed away which impacted my research in 2013. In 2014, I realized that I needed to record all of the things that I have discovered from my research up to 2011, from the 2011 trip, and since the trip. I need to record the memories, the stories, the questions, and the conclusions. I would absolutely hate for my children to have to start over at square one because I didn't take the time to record my discoveries. If I am never able to share those stories, at least they'll be in square two or three because the things I know are preserved, recorded, and accessible to them.

Share

How long after you die will anyone living have a personal memory of you? Andy, my husband, met two of his great grandmothers when he was young. The last one died in 1990. Andy, his brothers, and cousins are the last generation with a memory of these ladies. They are only three generations removed. He does have written accounts of ancestors who are much older, from the 1600s and 1700s.

In contrast, most of my great-grandparents died in the 1930s and 1940s. My last surviving great-grandparent passed away in the early 1970s before I was born. I have no living memory of these relatives that are only three generations back. Additionally, I have no memory of one of my grandparents, as he died when I was young. I have a handful of stories of my ancestors, but they only go back into the 1800s.

If we have few memories of the people only three generations back, how can we possibly have stories from people we've never met? The ancestor, or some other family member, took the time to write out a little bit about their life. Some of these handwritten accounts were published in books which are long since out of print. In the digital age, those words have been immortalized. Images of the books and even original handwritten letters are digitized and shared. While no one living remembers the long departed ancestors, records of their lives will continue to endure for generations.

The question you must ask yourself is, "What's the point of doing family history research if you are not going to pass along your findings?" Having discovered, organized, and recorded your family members' stories, you will want to share your findings.

Identify the Goal

We discussed in a previous chapter on the importance of defining your goals in relation to your research objectives. Preparing to share stories also starts with a goal. When you have goals in mind, they will guide you in developing and creating your presentations. If your goal was to extend your family tree, your presentation could be a family tree either in a printed or an artistic format. If your goal was a biographical sketch, you have more options with the information you found on one individual than just a 300-word essay submitted to a newsletter. Keep your goals in mind as you review this chapter. Perhaps one of these larger formats will be well suited for your purposes.

Who Do You Want To Include?

The project you wish to share with your family can be loosely categorized into five types:

1. *Individuals* - the focus is on a single person. Think of this as a biography. It could also be a collection of 'sayings' or stories from that particular person, which is less biographical but is certainly

still focused. Other family members' stories may be included as they interact with the individual.

2. *Families* - the focus is on a family. For instance, my immediate family publishes a book each year about our daily lives. It's part journal, part photo album. Compiling this book involves all of the members of a family and includes events that everyone participated in. We also include individual events that help to tell what that family member was doing in the overall family story.

3. *Superfamilies* - Another format would be to focus on a few generations of related families in a particular geographic area. The area may have had a lot of intermarriages, so you end up with one superfamily. Many early county histories end up being superfamilies.

4. *Ancestors* - Pick a starting person and go backward in time as far as you want. Keep in mind, the farther back in time you research, the more daunting the task.

5. *Descendants* - Pick a person or couple and go forward in time through their children, grandchildren, and so on.

For the ancestral and descendant project, attempt 7 or more generations only if you have others helping you. Each generation has twice as many people as the previous generation. The 7th generation has 128 parents, and there could be hundreds of more children to include as well. Your project increases exponentially in complexity and scope of research as you add more generations of ancestors.

 # You'll have more success with smaller projects in the beginning.

Who Is The Project For?

You consulted your interests and abilities when starting this family history adventure. When you consider how to present what you have found, consider the interest and needs of others. Understand your audience for the project before diving into the presentation format. Each kind of audience will have different needs and desires to appreciate your efforts.

Your audience can be categorized in the following ways:

1. *Immediate family* - These are the people that you know the best, so you will know what they are going to be most interested in. You will be able to include very personal stories that aren't meant to be shared outside of the family. For example, our yearly family history books are intended for our immediate family. As such, we can include stories that have significant meaning for us that we wouldn't necessarily want everyone to read.

2. *Extended family* - The people you are related to. They are going to be the group most interested in your research. Your project can be a way to help them know you or your common ancestors bet-

ter. You wouldn't want to share every story possible with them, but you can share more than larger audiences would bear to suffer through.

3. *Targeted group* - This could take any number of forms. You might be writing about an individual who was the president of an organization, so you would expect that organization to be most interested in the stories. It could be a superfamily history about the founding of a city. Many other possibilities exist. You must keep in mind this specific group and tailor the presentation with them in mind. They will enjoy stories that relate their association to your family member. This audience may not want all the daily life details.

4. *General public* - The final category is for everyone (although most people probably won't be interested). Remember that this audience will need explanations. Include explanations for words, phrases, or sayings that are not in common usage. (While many in Texas should know what "gigging" is, people in New York most likely do not. Google the term if you do not know.) Acronyms, local history, and geography all should be described so that a reader can understand, regardless of the background he or she is coming from. Additionally, the general public has a shorter attention span. They only have time for stories that have an emotional appeal or

are the most entertaining. Share less with the general public than with your closest relatives. Also write your stories on a 6th-9th-grade level as few will appreciate a large vocabulary or grammatical style. Finally, general public projects must respect privacy and treat sensitive topics with delicacy. Not all details of your family should be shared with a mass audience, for the sake of maintaining family harmony.

 # Don't aim for awards/wealth. Strive for legacy preservation.

Make a Plan

Once you have answered these two important questions (who to include and who is it for), then you can start to put together a plan. It doesn't have to be written out, although for large projects you might consider it. What kinds of things do we need to include in a plan?

About 20 years ago, my husband's Aunt Gloria had a vision. His extended family gathered for a reunion to celebrate his grandparents 50th anniversary. All of their eight children and all but one of their 28 living grandchildren were there. For their 60th anniversary, Gloria wanted it to be even better!

Her vision was to compile a family history, written by everyone. She would have the books printed and ready to hand out at the family reunion. More than a year before the reunion Gloria laid out her plan. She provided everyone with a list of topics that they could write about each month to help us along. She left the content decisions to each of the adult children and grandchildren to determine what to write about and how much.

The deadline for the histories was six months before the anniversary. Andy, my husband, had every intention of taking the full year to craft out a nice complete story of his life. However, life got in the way - including graduating from college and welcoming our first child into the world. The deadline came and went. A week after the deadline, he panicked. Andy didn't want to be told that Gloria was waiting on him. He did a quick mental calculation of how many people might be contributing and how long his part should be. Andy decided that five pages would be enough. The weekend after the deadline, he punched out five pages about his life. After all, he is the expert on his life.

Andy emailed his contribution to Gloria hoping that she would forgive the tardiness. He was in for a big surprise. A week later, the family received a mass email from Aunt Gloria, gently chastising everyone for not finishing their histories by the deadline. She commented about how much work putting the book together was going to be and the importance of getting everything in so that it could be edited. It wasn't just a few family members who hadn't finished or even several. It was all of them, except, for Andy. Gloria expressed heartfelt thanks to him for being on time, though he knew he was late.

Ten years later, his family created an addendum to the first project. Andy turned his portion in a month ahead of time and was again surprised to be the first one done. I guess his family likes to wait until after the last minute.

Plan the Scope

How long do you want your project to be? Are you making a scrapbook, a pamphlet, a collection of short stories, or a memoir? Are you going to make a 5-minute audio recording, a 10-minute slideshow, or an hour long documentary?

Before deciding upon the length of your project, investigate what information is available. If you skipped the discovery and recording phases discussed in Chapters 1 and 3, you need to go back before you go forward.

Don't be surprised if your initial estimate is off. Aunt Gloria was expecting 250-300 pages for her project. She ended up with more than 600 pages! I had enough information to complete a 50-page scrapbook featuring my mother. Instead, I limited myself to 30 pages. Andy and I do not set a limit on our yearly personal history project. We have yet to exceed 200 pages, so that is feasible for us. For annual videos we have made, we limited our project to 2 hours as that was all our DVDs could hold with high quality.

Start small. A bunch of small projects can be combined later to make a large one. If you want to create a large project, be sure to get help from others.

What Tasks Need To Be Done?

By this phase, you will have little research to do. But as you create the project, you might find unanswered questions that need to be researched. Each project may require written stories (even if they are spoken in an audio or video project). With any presentation style, editing and formatting will be a critical step. You will need to organize the materials you will use for the particular project. Hopefully, you have already organized your collection of possessions and are only pulling out what is needed for each specific project. The type of project you choose will have additional tasks that must be done. Create a list of all the tasks that need to be done. As you do this more and more, you will become better acquainted with what you need to have done and how detailed your to-do list needs to be.

When Do You Want to Have It Completed?

One of the biggest obstacles to creating family history projects is constantly thinking that we need to add something more. These are peoples' lives. There are thousands of pertinent facts, hundreds of stories for each person's life. Accept that you can't include everything.

Set a date of when you want your project finished, and lay out a schedule with the list of tasks. These dates become your deadlines. If you can't find your 4th great grandfather's birth date by your deadline, then it won't go in this family history presentation. Don't let perfection get in the way of completing your project. You can always update later.

Who Do You Need to Help With It?

If Aunt Gloria had tried writing her family history book all by herself, it would never have been completed. There are 28 individuals that she would need to interview and write about. It was much easier just to have the individual family members write their personal history. Most people can't fathom writing a 300-page family history, but they can see themselves writing 2 to 10 pages about their life or a close relative's life. Divide up the work and solicit others to help you. At the very least, your family should review what you've created to ensure accuracy before the final product is made available for all.

What format do you want this to take?

Will your project present a collection of facts, stories, or a mix of both? If you want to publish facts, do not kill trees for boring books.

Give up the idea of printing a book of family group records and pedigree charts! Although these books contain important information, they are absolutely boring to the vast majority of people. Additionally, with modern technology, printing such a project is a waste of money as the information can be more affordably and efficiently shared using databases, online trees, or websites.

Instead of producing charts, share stories. Don't limit your stories to printed formats. Video and audio presentations may be more appealing and reach a much larger audience.

Your formats will most likely fit into these categories:

1. *Biographical narrative* - whether you are sharing a printed or recorded life sketch, a biographical presentation is far better than facts on a chart. Listen to the *"Stuff You Missed in History Class"* podcast to understand the power of biographies to entertain and enlighten and model your narratives in that manner (without the ad breaks).

2. *Developed narrative* - This format reads like a nonfiction book or a well-written biography. The facts are all there, but put in the context of a story (remember, we humans love stories). Be aware though that this type of book is the most difficult and time-consuming to write well. If written poorly, your reader is going to put it down. I wouldn't recommend this type for your first large project. Start with a short life sketches.

3. *History compilation* - The family history books that Aunt Gloria compiles is a combination of generic historical information in the first part, individuals family histories in the second part (which were all written in different styles), and finally family group sheets at the end. If you keep family groups sheets to less than 10% of your printed project, the charts become helpful reference tools to assess relationships quickly. If the compilation is only group sheets and pedigree charts, leave them on a computer or online tree.

4. *Story Collection* - My great-uncle served in World War II, and he would share stories of the war at the family events. One year, his grandson decided that he'd listen to Grandpa Bill's stories and record them. He compiled these stories into a small booklet with photos of Grandpa Bill at that time in his life. Little

energy is spent on the full life of Bill, but his stories, often retold among family members, are now preserved for future generations.

5. ***Quotes Collection*** - Gather the sayings a person is known for and sharing them. The inclusion of the meaning behind the 'isms' and the impact those sayings have had on different family members would enrich the collection. My friend's father had a lot of memorable sayings. She'll say them often beginning with, "My daddy always used to say...." The next time she catches herself saying a "Daddy says," she should record them and what they mean to her.

6. ***Poem, Essay, or Song Collection*** - Perhaps your family member was talented. Perhaps they wrote poetry or short essays. Gathering these together would be of great value to family members, and perhaps a larger audience if the appeal is broad. Perhaps your relative was a talented musician. They may never have an opportunity to produce an album for mass audiences, but the recording of their vocal or musical abilities would be priceless to their descendants.

Andy has a collection of essays that he submitted for English classes in high school. He is super smart (yes, I'm rather biased) but he just didn't like spending his time reading something he considered boring. What was boring? Anything by Jane Austen or the Bronte sisters topped the list. His essays would be well written but not reflect the assignment his teacher desired. His infamous essay was the "Rollerblade Conspiracy" about why he was unable to read and write an essay about *Jane Eyre*. He has compiled these essays, the teacher's comments, and the back story for the essays in a book *How to Fail English With Style.* Our family loves having this collection and the back story to say, "That's our Andy!"

7. **Letters** - Many people have a collection of letters exchanged between family members, especially sweethearts, during wars or after moving distances away. Consider sharing the letters in a series of videos or a book. You can have a male voice and a female voice read the letter exchange if the letter writers are no longer able to do it themselves. In the midst of the exchanges, you can include the background information that is hinted at in the exchange but not specifically explained.

8. **Journals** - Many people have preserved journals from various family members. Journals can provide wonderful historical information for history researchers. They can also provide rich depth to the lives of ancestors. Consider publishing a journal so that the words can be reviewed by many, rather than just the person who owns the original. Include images of the original handwriting and the transcriptions (or translation if it was written in a different language). You can add photos and additional commentary to better explain the journal entries.

9. **Reflections** - When you discover your family or rediscover your personal history, many thoughts come to mind. There are so many lessons that I have learned from my family history: Lessons about doing my duty, continuing on no matter what life throws at me, and the damage alcoholism and abuse can do to a family for generations to come. There are reflections from my own life, mistakes that I hope my family

never has to repeat. There are thoughts on the good choices I have made and where that has led me in my life as well. A reflections project can detail these things I hope I have learned and want to pass on to my children and grandchildren.

10. *Historical Fiction* - Perhaps you are rather creative and can invent dialogue and scenery when none currently exists in sources contemporary to the lives of your family member. Perhaps you can find the drama and the resolution that is worth telling. If so, you may consider using your family members' lives as the foundation for a historical fiction or a 'based on a true story' project. Be sure you respect the living family members you include in such works. Even though your book is fiction, if someone can identify a living individual in the book based on your description and life events, you can still injure that person and those around them. Also, be sure the reader knows that this is fiction based on true facts so they don't incorrectly read the book as complete fact.

11. *Other* - Perhaps your relative had paintings, recipes, handicrafts, or collections ranging from Coca Cola items to movie star plates. If that is the case, you might want to share these collections in a variety of formats. Many of these items would need visual media, but not necessarily. You could create a cooking show based on the recipes, or compile a recipe book. You can create a slideshow or photo book featuring the handicrafts, listing the materials used and the stories behind the creations. Perhaps you are really crafty, and you can combine some photos and make a new artistic creation. At the end of each school year, I scan all of my kids' artwork and other projects. I then

print a book that displays these items. It sure does help in keeping my refrigerator tidy.

Did you noticed that wide variety of formats available? This list is far from exhaustive. Don't let this list stifle your project inspiration. Be creative. Be innovative. Have fun.

Take time to consider your audience and let them guide your decisions in determine what to share and how to do it.

What are Other Sharing Options?

Modern genealogy has brought us many mediums through which we can share our stories and remember our ancestors:

- **Printed projects: written histories, scrapbooks, biographical directories**

- **Digitized projects: e-books, digital photo albums photo sharing websites, slideshows, videos**

- **Shared articles with Genealogical Societies**

- **Donated family histories to a History Library**

- **Written blog posts**

- **Shared videos on YouTube**

- **Shared photos/stories on FamilySearch/Ancestry**

- **Shared research files through DVD or the cloud**

Notice how this list includes options that deliver your stories, no matter if they are large projects or smaller ones. Depending upon which project format and delivery method you choose, you can create great excitement for the history of your family among your other family members. Or, you might be able to give pieces of a story to someone who can pull all those pieces together into a project of their own.

What Other Resources Do You Need?

If you are collaborating with others, then you might try an online application like Google Docs or FastPencil so that everyone can have access to it. Technology is a great way to get the younger generation involved in family history. They are growing up with it and will need to use these skills in future jobs. They probably know more about it then you do. If they don't, you can encourage them to learn with a specific task.

 **Share your plan with those who are going to help or are in your target audience.**

You will be surprised who would be willing to edit a few chapters of your family history, watch a video, or listen to an audio clip for the sole purpose of helping you present a fabulous final product. Let people volunteer for assignments.

Everyone isn't going to want to do everything. Think of creating your family history project as a team sport, with you as the coach. You may not be able to throw a 30-yard pass, but you can identify someone who can and have that person throw the passes. Meanwhile, let others block and another run. You need staff on the sidelines for medical emergencies. Even the lowly waterboy has an important job.

Don't try to do this project alone. Again, even the scrimmage's audience has the critical role of providing feedback before something is presented en masse.

Aunt Gloria was the coach for the extensive family history volumes. It certainly didn't mean that she was able to sit back and relax. More likely, she was the only one who had an idea of what the finished product was going to be. Lots of family members helped with writing, some helped with editing, and others worked with the photos. Through it all, Gloria coached the team to victory.

Execute Your Plan

Now that you have defined what you want to do, who is going to help, and what other resources are needed, its time to put the plan into action. Your project may be completed in an afternoon or it may take years.

Using the example of Andy's aunt, she probably spent four solid months compiling everything and getting it ready for printing. Previous to that she had spent time the year before publication trying to prepare everyone for the task. Thankfully, the second time around she had some experience under her belt and knew what needed to get done when. Even still she spent a considerable amount of time on volume 2 of our family stories.

 **It only take three generations before memories vanish without a trace if family history isn't purposefully recorded and shared.**

Take time to share your discoveries and research. Perhaps we can change the sad truth that "Gone But Not Forgotten" too many times is a bald faced lie. Combine the different parts (photo, possessions, and people) with the writings or audio recordings into a captivating, and enjoyable story.

You will be able to share your family history in a way that is enjoyable and more like a historical novel than a textbook. You can then present your very real, very personal stories using old photos and documents, in much the same way the television show *Who Do You Think You Are?* does.

Those you share your discoveries and recordings with will be able to experience the wide range of emotions and weird coincidences that make up a family's narrative. Those you share with will laugh. They will cry. They will be disappointed. Occasionally, they may be honored to be related to the people they call family. They will have their champions (and their villains). And what's the hook? Your passion about your discoveries.

reimagine Family History

Having read this book, you should have a new vision of family history. It's more than just name collecting and tree climbing. If you want to achieve those goals, press on, they are part of the overarching subject of family history. Know that if you will discover where your history is hiding in your home, organize the content you have so it will be salvaged from the trash heap, and record your findings to share with others, you are doing genealogy the right way, right now. You will go further, faster in family history than almost anyone else and you'll have more fun along the way.

People take up hobbies and pastimes because they gain enjoyment and relaxation from them. Family history should not be drudgery. It should encompass what you want to do. As with other popular pursuits, this should be something you define. Reimagine what family history can entail for you.

Understanding the lives of your ancestors' has the power to strengthen you, your children, and generations to come. Enjoy the journey. There is always going to be something more you can do but the journey is not about what is waiting for you on the other side of a brick wall. It's about the stories of your family and how their lives shaped who they were and you are today.

About the Authors

Devon Noel Lee specializes in preserving and sharing family memories and motivating budding genealogists. She has created and published 60 scrapbooks, written a memoir from her teenage years and four family history how-to books, including the popular *A Recipe for Writing Family History*. She has written the stories for over 120 ancestors and counting and is working on compiling many of them into a book. Devon is a high energy speaker and lab instructor at local, state, national genealogy conferences and public libraries. She educates and inspires the genealogy world through videos at FamilyHistoryFanatics.com. This former beauty queen reported on pageant news for 16 years. She graduated from Texas A&M with degrees in Marketing and Journalism. Currently, Devon is a home educator for five superheroes.

Andy Lee has been involved in family history for 30 years and wrote a contest winning essay about an American Revolution ancestor while in high school. As a member of Toastmaster's International, Andy has achieved the status of Competent Communicator and won several storytelling contests. He has given presentations throughout the US and Canada to professional organizations, university classes, local genealogy societies, family history conferences, and Boy Scout organizations. Andy's topics range beyond genealogy to include engineering, problem-solving, finances, business building and emergency preparedness. He's the co-author of *A Recipe for Writing Family History* and contributes to the FamilyHistoryFanatics.com YouTube channel. Andy graduated from Texas A&M University with a degree in Mechanical Engineering.